Success Isn't A Problem, Our Ignorance Is

Magan Kalra

Copyright © 2022 by Magan Kalra

All rights reserved. This book or any portion thereof may not be reproduced or used in any manner whatsoever without the express written permission of the respective writer of the respective poem/story except for the use of brief quotations in a book review. The writer of the respective work holds sole responsibility for the originality of the poems/stories and The Write Order is not responsible in any way whatsoever.

Printed in India

ISBN: 978-93-95079-19-8

Second Printing, 2022

The Write Order

Koramangala, Bangalore

Karnataka-560029

THE WRITE ORDER PUBLICATIONS.

www. thewriteorder. com

Dedication

I lovingly dedicate this book to my Dad, and to my Son.

TABLE OF CONTENTS

Introduction 1

CHAPTER 1 13
Successful People Do Not Under-Estimate Their Potential

CHAPTER 2 25
Successful People Do Not Let The Fire In Them Extinguish

CHAPTER 3 35
Successful People Are Not Self-Centered

CHAPTER 4 47
Successful People Do Not Expect Results Without Action

CHAPTER 5 57
Successful People Do Not Fight Symptoms

Chapter 6 65
Successful People Are Not Rigid In Their Thinking

BONUS CHAPTERS

Bonus Chapter 7 81
Successful People Do Not Get Disillusioned By The Comfort Of Smart Work

Bonus Chapter 8 99
Successful People Do Not Give Up

BLOGS

BLOG 1 115
8 Great Words Of Wisdom From Movies

Blog 2 121
(Right) Practice Makes A (Wo)Man Perfect

Blog 3 129
10 Habits Of Successful Entrepreneurs

Conclusion 139

Acknowledgement 141

INTRODUCTION

Why does success seem so elusive?

What stops you from succeeding?

Why does it seem that success favours certain individuals and bypasses many others?

What makes a Bill Gates, a JK Rowling, a Steve Jobs, an Amitabh Bachchan, a Dhiru Bhai Ambani or an Oprah Winfrey? What separates these massively successful personalities from common folk?

Why is it that some people keep struggling and to others success comes with ease?

The answer is straight forward and not necessarily easily digestible- "Success isn't a problem, our ignorance is." When you own up to your own ignorance magic begins to happen.

Ever since the dawn of civilization philosophers, thinkers, saints and practically everyone who has ever wanted to do anything on this planet, has wondered, why is success so difficult to catch?

The concept of success has always fascinated mankind. It has been the same for me. Multiple success masters and authors have studied thousands of successful individuals to know exactly what they do. Endless number of studies on the same are being conducted right now as you read this book.

When you observe these giants closely, you will find that they have developed their lifestyles, their habits and their mental dispositions in such a way that it seems that success for them is on autopilot.

One of the most fascinating discoveries is that when these success masters from different regions of the world compare their findings with each other, all their findings tally. That is, a successful person in America or Switzerland pretty much does the same things and has more or less the same worldview as a successful person in India or Sweden, or even in Somalia.

In my experience too, I see it so very evidently, almost every day. My profession has given me an opportunity to interact with some extraordinary achievers across the globe. Well, my observation: no matter what country I go to, all of them have similar habits that have made them who they are. And guess what those similar habits are... they all avoid the same pitfalls, regardless of their country of origin or residence, the education they've had, the background they come from or the kind of businesses they run.

The beauty of this pattern is its universal applicability. Even cosmic.

The good news is, we now know, why certain individuals succeed, and certain individuals don't.

It's almost like a formula.

You can call it an algorithm, or even a mathematical equation. If you provide the right guideline to solve this equation, success is guaranteed.

This is neither a scientific invention nor fiction. It is a conclusion based on solid empirical data gathered over centuries.

Though, it is very important to know exactly what needs to be done to achieve success, it is equally important to know what not to do. This book reveals what successful people don't do. Successful people avoid some pitfalls, so that what they do, becomes a lot more effective. Imagine, you start exercising to stay fit, you start dieting too, but you continue to overindulge in alcohol, desserts, etc. Would exercise be effective? Would dieting be effective? Would you be successful in achieving your goal?

My endeavour through this book is to share with you those pitfalls that create hurdles on your way to success.

What is it that successful people strictly avoid?

These mental attitudes and everyday habits counter every positive effort with negative outfalls. Unless you avoid these pitfalls, you will take one step forward and two steps backward. No matter how hard you try, unless you get rid of your negative habits and misplaced notions, you're not going to succeed.

In the following chapters I have shared six things that you should refrain from doing if you want to be successful in your life or in your business.

Why six and why not 10 or 20?

The number doesn't really matter. I was instinctively making a list of things that I have observed successful people avoid and I was able to pack the entire gist within six. These six chapters are the focal points. You can expand them or contract them in a way you feel convenient. Every chapter deals with one trap each that you MUST avoid.

So, here is the first trap you should avoid in order to be successful.

CHAPTER 1

Successful People Do Not Under-Estimate Their Potential

"You are confined only by the walls you build (around) yourself."

-Andrew Murphy

Successful People Do Not Under-Estimate Their Potential

Life is difficult – this is the belief I was raised with, but somewhere I could never really digest it. I had this undeniable urge to prove that this ideology, this thinking is very limiting, very disempowering. I always felt that this is not something that I agree with, and I wanted to break free. I remember reading a story about a bumblebee.

You know, according to the theory of aerodynamics, the bumblebee should not be able to fly, but the bumblebee doesn't know this, and it flies anyway. When I learned this, I was liberated. I just knew that I can have anything in my life as long as I am willing to earn it.

One day my son came to me and said, Papa you keep telling me that I can have anything in my life, is this really true? I said yes, my son, you can have anything as long as you're willing to earn it. So, he said that means I can even get on an aeroplane. I said-of course you can. He said, no, I am not talking about a toy plane, I am talking about a real plane. I said-of course you can get a real plane, you can get anything, anything-as long as you're willing to earn it! Imagine, if we can raise our children with this belief, what would be possible for them, how would their life be, what impact it would have on the generations to come.

The point is, you have to decide exactly what you want in your life, and then you must determine the price you're going to have to pay in order to get what you want and then resolve to pay that price.

But that price must be paid in advance because we reap exactly what we sow, but we must sow first. The secret is this- Success only comes after we've paid the price never before and in my experience across the world, training and coaching some wonderful people, people who are self-made, are the ones who decided what they wanted, and then they had to earn it, nothing came on the platter. This is true for me. Think about it, I am sure whatever you've achieved in your life, whatever you've done so far is a function of your hard work. It's the function of you really-really-really wanting it and then willing to put in whatever work required to get that and that is the mantra. You can have anything in your life as long as you're willing to earn it.

As kids, we look at the world like a place full of opportunities and consider ourselves formidable, but over the years, from external as well as internal feedback, we build an opinion about ourselves and unfortunately, this opinion is often negative. We develop the notion that it is not easy to succeed, life is tough. We don't have what it takes, we are incapable.

Some of the misplaced notions, or negative beliefs or disempowering thoughts that you may have developed over the years are:

- Life is difficult
- I don't know enough
- I am not lucky
- It's not easy
- I never got an opportunity
- I didn't get the right guidance
- I am not as smart as others
- I am not as intelligent as others
- I don't have enough resources
- People aren't fair to me
- God isn't fair to me
- I know am going to fail
- It's not my cup of tea, I can't do this
- It's not in my destiny

Imagine an open field, bedded with green grass. You start walking on one particular part of that field. You walk on the same part every day for days, weeks, months, years. What would start to emerge after sometime?

You will see a clear trail emerging. This is also how neurons in our brain function. When you keep repeating any thought, any belief whether positive or negative as I mentioned earlier, your brain starts to accept them as the truth, and a clear path to failure or success is built. These are a bunch of excuses that we make over time. We even gather enough evidence to prove them real. This is the quickest way to an unsuccessful, frustrated life. Sad, but true. Confronting, but true.

Successful people dismantle these false, made-up beliefs. These are the mental walls you have built around yourself. You have to unshackle yourself from the chains of under-confidence. You have to set aside your fear of failure.

You will be pleasantly surprised to know that you are more capable than you can ever imagine. Our brain is so powerful that many of us may argue that we already know this, but the fact is that you know it only at an intellectual level and knowing anything only at an intellectual level is insufficient when it comes to building a successful life. I have already mentioned, it's the combination of external and internal feedback that wreaks havoc.

As children we don't carry that baggage. And whatever we do, we do it with wonderment and with unbridled confidence. As we grow, we start receiving negative feedback. We start

Successful People Do Not Under-Estimate Their Potential

experiencing the stigma that's attached to failure.

As we grow, we begin to accumulate all sorts of doubts about ourselves. We begin to think that we know less. We begin to think that we are less capable than those who succeed.

What really separates super achievers from underachievers? It's not that successful people don't have these fears or doubts. It's how they deal with those fears and doubts.

Once in an interview Sachin Tendulkar shared that whenever he opened the innings, he felt as scared as the first time in his career, every time.

He didn't play without fear, he simply conquered that fear. Just imagine had he given in to the fear he would never have become what he eventually became. Would Indian cricket be the same? Would we know him as the God of cricket? He faced his fear.

There are multiple ways you can do the same. Here are the three ways that have worked well for me:

The first way is to simply stop doubting yourself. Drop it, because this tunnel has no cheese. Stop it because you don't want to sweat the small stuff, and it is all small stuff.

The second way is to seek the opinion of someone you trust. If you really feel that you lack a particular piece of knowledge, then gain that knowledge. Make an objective list of your abilities and strengths and make note of the gaps that you need to fill and then start filling those gaps. Stop thinking and start acting.

To do this well and fast, I recommend that you get a coach for yourself. A coach is able to look at you, your situation and your challenges by being completely detached from them. A coach can hold you accountable, at the same time enabling you and empowering you to move towards your goals by taking very objective and meaningful actions.

I say this because I have experienced this first hand. In fact, very early in my childhood.

I come from a very small town in Haryana called Bhiwani. We had to move to Delhi after my dad passed away. When we relocated, it wasn't just a different city, for me it was moving to a completely different orbit.

At that time, I couldn't even speak a word of English, so making friends wasn't easy, I had a low self-esteem, and that became a huge barrier for me because I wasn't getting accepted in any of the schools.

It wasn't only about the language, I did not have the confidence to speak to people and without even realizing I began to under-estimate myself, my potential.

I am not good enough, I held that belief for a very long time. The angel coach came to me in the form of my sister, and she helped me overcome that belief. She had moved to Delhi before I did, and she could very objectively and holistically look at the challenges I was facing. She started coaching me. Her style was very simple, practical and untraditional.

I distinctly remember, she would give me five sentences to memorize every day. She asked me categorically to practise those sentences while I spoke to anybody. When I did what she had suggested, I experienced a shift in my confidence, at least for those five sentences.

Oftentimes I used those sentences out of context and thus was laughed at. But she kept encouraging me and made me feel as if I was doing it on my own.

The way it exists for me now is, as if one morning I woke up and I could simply speak the language. It was magical! The reason it seems magical is because she made the journey easy for me and this would not have been possible without my sister.

The third thing you must do is, learn to embrace failure. Or else don't do anything and you will never fail.

Remember, what you do with your potential, is what it does for you.

You've read the chapter, you can relate to the examples from your own life, now what?

Now, ACT

Acknowledge. **C**ontemplate. **T**ake Action.

And here's what you can do immediately to bring about a powerful lasting result:

Acknowledge:
In which areas of your life have you been under-estimating your potential and how?

_____

_____

_____

Contemplate:
In what ways has it impacted: you? Write at least one word each in the columns below:

Impact on Myself	
Impact on My Health	
Impact on My Goals	
Impact on My Family	
Impact on My Work	

Take responsibility:

Top three actions that you can take immediately that will bring the significant positive change to this area:

Action Step 1:	
Action Step 2:	
Action Step 3:	

CHAPTER 2

Successful People Do Not Let The Fire In Them Extinguish

"A burning desire to be, and to do, is the starting point from which the dreamer must take off. Dreams are not born of indifference, laziness or lack of ambition."

– Napoleon Hill

When success is just wishful thinking, it remains a wishful thinking. Success is a serious business. You cannot succeed by simply wishing to succeed. You have to give it your sweat and blood. You have to invest in success. Success only comes after you've paid the price, never before.

But for that to happen, you have to have a burning desire. You cannot give all to your pursuit if there is no burning desire. You cannot authentically up your stakes merely at the wishful thinking level.

You must have heard the story of Dashrath Manjhi? A Bollywood film was made on him. Dashrath Manjhi was a poor farmer from a village in Bihar. He worked across a mountain and everyday his wife used to bring food to him after crossing the mountain. Once, while crossing the mountain, she fell and later succumbed to her injuries. She couldn't be taken to the hospital because there was no direct way to it. In order to reach the hospital, one had to cross the mountain.

Enraged and in deep grief, Dashrath Manjhi decided to carve a way through the mountain so that the people of his village could get easier access to the hospital. It took him 22 years to create a road through the massive rock. People called him mad but that only strengthened his resolve. He created the passage between 1960-83.

Due to his effort, the distance people had to cover to reach the Gaya district was reduced from 55 km to 15 km. He used just a hammer and chisel.

His story might be a bit of a stretch, but could he have done what he did without a burning desire? When you examine this carefully, you will realize that Dashrath Manjhi took on a purpose that was bigger than himself, it wasn't a selfish purpose, but a purpose that impacted a larger community. He had a vision. A clear resolve. Above all, he had a burning desire, he had a stand in the matter.

A burning desire keeps you going. A burning desire makes you look for solutions rather than getting turned off by problems. When you have a burning desire, excuses don't bog you down. Even when you are faced with obstacles, your burning desire gives you the strength to dismantle the obstacles and move ahead.

But a burning desire doesn't come from thin air. It has to be backed by a strong sense of purpose. You need to find the "why" of what you really want to do.

Have you heard of Abhishek Sunil Thaware? He is India's first and up till now the only teeth archer. In the absence of an arm or in the absence of a working arm a teeth archer pulls the arch with his or her teeth in order to shoot it.

Negligence by doctors who were treating him for simple fever gave him polio in his right arm but instead of hurling himself into the crater of his misfortune, he found a purpose in life. He found a "why" for himself. He wanted to serve his country. He wanted to make India proud.

Sports was his call. He started participating in various athletic events and he competed in many State level and National level sports events. The destiny had decided to be more tough with him.

Due to an injury in the knee ligament leg, the doctors advised him never to participate in athletics. Instead of giving up, he took up teeth archery because for that one doesn't have to run and jump around. One of his friends was a renowned archer and he took inspiration from him.

If he hadn't lost his arm to polio, he would have joined the defence services and in fact, that was his dream as a child. He wanted to serve his country (his ultimate "why"). He didn't give up. As they say, where there is a will, there is a way. He found that way in teeth archery.

So far, Abhishek has excelled at the Para Archery World Championship Trials conducted by the Archery Association of India. He bagged a silver medal at the All-India Archery Meet for the disabled in Baroda. He also qualified for a state-level meet (where the able-bodied would compete) conducted by the Nagpur District Association. In Solapur he finished 27th in the state archery meet. In Nagpur University's college meet he scored 637/720 points. In Patiala, competing with able-bodied archers at the Inter-University meet, out of 200 participants, he took the 69th spot. He gave a tough competition to archers with both hands.

Do you think Abhishek could have achieved all this without a burning desire to serve his country? His ultimate aim is to get a gold medal for the country in the Olympics. Even in the case of Darshrath Manjhi, initially the trigger might have been the grief and the anger of losing his wife, but eventually, the "why" turned into a larger purpose of making life easier for the villagers. Unless, you have a burning desire to succeed, you are not going to succeed. You have to find what drives you, what motivates you, and if it is at the level of a burning desire, then that's the beginning of your success journey.

> *"Success only comes after you've paid the price, never before."*
>
> *– Magan Kalra*

You've read the chapter, you can relate to the examples from your own life, now what?

Now, ACT

Acknowledge. **C**ontemplate. **T**ake Action.

And here's what you can do immediately to bring about a powerful lasting result:

Acknowledge:
In which areas of your life do you not feel fired up? Write at least three examples.

_____

_____

_____

Contemplate:
In what ways has it impacted: you? Write at least one word each in the columns below:

Impact on Myself	
Impact on My Health	
Impact on My Goals	
Impact on My Family	
Impact on My Work	

Take responsibility:

Top three actions that you can take immediately that will bring the significant positive change to this area:

Action Step 1:	
Action Step 2:	
Action Step 3:	

CHAPTER 3

Successful People Are Not Self-Centred

"You can get everything in life you want, if you will just help enough other people get what they want."

– Zig Ziglar

When I was in school, I had a subject called social studies, and for some reason one sentence that I always remembered from the curriculum book was that "man is a social animal." This means, by nature, we are all social beings. We thrive when we work together. There is solid research data that shows when you contribute to the success of others, you may not get an immediate reward, but in the long run, it pays off.

Unfortunately, while trying to pursue our goals, or at least when we think that we are pursuing our goals, we forget this central characteristic of humanity. We become too self-centred. We become islands.

Now, to a certain degree, being self-centred isn't bad. We need to have a self-preservation instinct. We shouldn't let others take advantage of ourselves and in the process, end up spending all the time doing others' work. Being taken advantage of is totally different from genuinely helping someone who really needs your help.

There were times in my life when I did not have any money.

And I remember, one of my friends (let's call him Ajay) came to me and asked me for it. The good one inside me woke up, and I said – "sure." I borrowed money from another friend of mine Ritesh Dahiya, (Dahiya ji as I fondly call him) and gave it to Ajay. When this became a pattern in my life, it obviously brought me under huge debt. This was plain-simple-stupid. Do not be stupid! Am not asking you to be stupid.

On the other hand, Dahiya ji knew how troubled I was and gave me enough time without even asking me for it. He never even asked me to return his money, because he loves me too much. I did return the money to him later. But Ajay never returned my money.

Fast forward 15 years, credit to social media, Ajay found my contact details and called me and spoke about the wonderful times and immediately asked me for help. He told me how difficult life is for him and asked me for money again. This time I said – "No." Simple. Some people may judge me on my decision. But this is not about right or wrong or good or bad.

The point is Ajay was self-centered.

Self-centred to the extent that when I had given him the money, I had even helped him get a job, enabling him to earn for himself, but he went absconding from that job too.

The point I am making is that being self-centered can only benefit you in the short-term, not in the long run.

I have had many Ajay's in my life, but I also have Dahiya ji. Dahiya ji and I do not talk often but I know that he knows that I love him, and I won't blink an eye to sacrifice my life for him. Dahiya ji is not self-centered.

Successful people are not self-centered.

Old habits die hard, but I also read somewhere, old habits hardly die. This morning my wife Gauri came to me and asked me to make a promise to her. She said, "Magan, promise me that you will stop lending money to just anybody without thinking because we have other commitments to fulfil this month." She continues to balance me and am still learning.

At the cost of repeating myself, don't be stupid.

The challenge with mankind today is that we are ready to step on others in order to move ahead. This mentality stems from the mindset of scarcity. You want to grab opportunities without sharing them with others because you feel that opportunities are scarce.

In fact, I have observed this behaviour in people almost 100%

of the time while conducting team and leadership workshops across the globe. Whenever we put people in different teams, invariably they assume each other as competitions and even get down to the lowest of the levels – not to win, but to make others lose. If Team A for some reason is not winning, they will ensure that Team B loses. This is a lose-lose mindset.

There's also a saying in Hindi – 'Hum to dubenge sanam, tumko bhi le dubenge.'

Another behaviour that I have often observed stems from the win: lose approach, which means if I have to win then the other person has to lose, this has been instilled in us since our childhood. But, if we truly want to grow and become successful, we have to take on a new approach, a win: win approach, where others don't have to lose for you to win. We can all be winners. You can win and I can win too. This is the abundance mindset, growth mindset, success mindset.

Both, the desire and courage to help others succeed comes from an abundance mentality. You help people because you know that there are limitless opportunities for everyone.

Helping others, without expecting returns brings you happiness and this has been proven scientifically. The medical profession has made a remarkable discovery through MRI technology. It has been discovered that helping others activates the same parts of the brain that are stimulated by food and even sex.

Here are some great benefits that successful people receive when they help others:

- They grow closer to like-minded people. They know just the way they help people; others would also help them back when needed.

- They develop a "confidence" mindset – helping others fills you with confidence. After all, you can help people only if you are capable.

- They spread a feeling of abundance – this is like the law of attraction. Whatever you send to the universe, the universe sends it back to you. When you are constantly using people without ever intending to help them, you attract the same sort of people and the same sort of circumstances. On the reverse, when you help people selflessly, you draw to yourself people who help you selflessly. Which in a lighter sense is also being selfish (and it's not always bad).

- Their perspective of life goes through a paradigm shift.

You begin to realise that money and career aren't everything although they are important for your success. This gives you a broader, a much wiser and a generous frame of mind and you can pursue success with greater degree of confidence and fulfilment.

And here's how it exactly pays you back in multiples:

1. Share opportunities: If you come across an opportunity that you can pass to others then you can help someone else benefit from it. People from different client organizations keep asking me to refer someone to them and there are people who get in touch with me because they are looking for a change, I help connect both. Many people have told me I should charge a recruitment fee for this. I simply smile and tell them that not everything needs to be charged for and it anyway comes back to me ten-folds. And my only investment was to think about who might be a good fit for the opportunity. All I had to do was forward an email or make a quick phone call. This simple act alone can turn into a blessing for someone else. And more often than not I have had the same people call me to offer a referral or a business opportunity that paid me back manifolds not only in terms of money, but also goodwill, credibility and reliable relationship network.

2. Share your knowledge: When you share your knowledge on a particular area that you are an expert on, you don't only help others, but you also help yourself by building your own brand in your area of expertise. I have done this many times by speaking at events free of charge, writing blogs filled with useful information and tips. I also provide no-obligation one-on-one coaching sessions to friends, family and business connections. When these people gain from you and experience a genuine you they come back and help you too.

3. Connect people: Most of us know people who can benefit from knowing each other, simply do that instead of keeping your connections to yourself.

Helping others may cost you little effort, but when you truly help someone, the chances are that it will pay you back hugely.

From an Indian context, Winston Churchill may not be an ideal person to quote, but here is something he once said that totally represents the central point of this chapter: "We make a living by what we get, we make a life by what we give."

You've read the chapter, you can relate to the examples from your own life, now what?

Now, ACT

Acknowledge. **C**ontemplate. **T**ake Action.

And here's what you can do immediately to bring about a powerful lasting result:

Acknowledge:
Can you recall in which areas of your life you've acted self - centered?

_____

_____

_____

Contemplate:
In what ways has it impacted: you? Write at least one word each in the columns below:

Impact on Myself	
Impact on My Health	
Impact on My Goals	
Impact on My Family	
Impact on My Work	

Take responsibility:

Top three actions that you can take immediately that will bring the significant positive change to this area:

Action Step 1:	
Action Step 2:	
Action Step 3:	

Success Isn't A Problem, Our Ignorance Is

CHAPTER 4

Successful People Do Not Expect Results Without Action

"Success is a function of persistence and doggedness and the willingness to work hard for 22 minutes to make sense of something that most people would give up on after 30 seconds."
– Malcolm Gladwell

You cannot reach your destination if you don't start moving. It doesn't matter how you move. But you have to move.

You can't keep lying in the bed, wishing that you were in the office, and then reach your office. Maybe in imagination you can achieve that, but in reality, you will need to make a physical effort.

Lemme share a story with you, once there was a man who wanted to pursue a spiritual path. Traditionally, it is believed that, pursuing a spiritual path means going into the forest, looking for a cave to sit and meditate. So, the man went off into the jungle, but of course he positioned himself close to his village because one needs food. So, the man sat in the jungle and kept reciting mantras, meditating and whenever he felt hungry he went to the village, begged for food and went back to the jungle. After a few days, as night fell, he noticed there was a fox, and both its front legs were severed in some trap or something. Fox had lost its legs, but it seemed to be well fed and healthy. Nature is not kind to any kind of incapability. If you lose your legs, you lose your life-that's the law of the jungle. But this fox had lost its legs and yet it was well fed and healthy. The man was surprised, but he ignored and focused on his meditation. As night fell, he heard the roar of a lion. He forgot about his meditation and climbed the tree. He sat there, and to his amazement, the lion, a full-grown male lion came with a piece of meat and dropped it in front of the fox and went away. The fox had its dinner, but he couldn't believe it. A crippled fox is being fed by a ferocious lion. For him it was a miracle! He felt this was a message from the divine. He kept wondering what it is that the divine wants him to get out of this incident. He kept wondering, kept thinking, and the next day again the lion came with a piece of meat and dropped it in front of the fox and went away. Now he was sure that God was sending a message to him but what is it, and then in his own way he interpreted the God's message, he said, "even a crippled fox in this forest is being fed by a lion, you fool why do you keep going and looking for food every day, just sit here and it will come and fall into your mouth." So he simply sat. One day, two days, three days passed and by the sixth day he was groaning between life and death. Another Yogi was passing that way and he heard the sound of this man groaning. He came towards the man and asked him "what happened to you? Why are you in this condition?"

The man replied, "Oh Yogi, please help me, a divine message came to me, I went by the message, and I became like this."

Successful People Don Not Expect Results Without Action

Yogi asked what do you mean, the man said look there, there's a crippled fox. Every day, that fox is being fed by a ferocious lion. Is this not God's message to me? Is this not a divine message?

The Yogi looked at him and said, "Definitely, this is a divine message, but why is it that you chose to be like a crippled fox and not like a generous lion?"

So, this is a choice that we have, every moment of our life, whatever the nature of the situations that we face, are you a generous lion or a crippled fox constantly waiting for miraculous results to happen in your favour without taking any action?

This holds true for every aspect of your life. The point is the result is a function of action. Period.

A wise person once said, "Success is when preparation meets opportunity," and this is so true. If you are not prepared, how can you benefit from the opportunity you come across?

Suppose you have always wanted to be a successful singer. But you don't practice every day. In fact, you rarely practice because you never expect to actually get an opportunity.

Then one day, you are attending a function and the lead singer who was supposed to perform at the function doesn't turn up. You can't make use of this opportunity because you are not prepared. Even when you try to perform, no one is impressed. Worse, a rep of a major label is also attending the function. If you were prepared, it could have been the best opportunity for you. And if you still don't learn from this predicament, you will blame your fate rather than yourself.

In "Outliers," Malcolm Gladwell says that on an average it takes 10,000 hours of serious practice to master a skill or an art. This, he found, holds true for every field, whether you want to become an expert pilot, a violinist, a doctor, a scientist, or a leader.

Although many efficiency experts have claimed that there are some exceptions to this "rule," the moot point is, if you want to succeed in life, if you really want to make a difference, you will have to make more effort than the average Joe.

If you need a professional degree for a promotion, get that degree instead of ruing the fact that your lack of qualification is putting hurdles in your way. If your skills are being replaced by computers, acquire new, contemporary and relevant skills. Computer programmers are always learning new programming languages or attending programming conventions because the old ones very quickly go obsolete. An average person gets lots of opportunities for success, but the problem is, very few people are well-equipped to benefit from, or even recognize those opportunities. Make an effort. If you fail, make an effort again. It's not about how much effort you have to put in, it's about how much you value what you want to achieve.

> "You have to sow the seed to enjoy the fruit, but you MUST SOW FIRST."
>
> – Magan Kalra

You've read the chapter, you can relate to the examples from your own life, now what?

Now, ACT

Acknowledge. **C**ontemplate. **T**ake Action.

And here's what you can do immediately to bring about a powerful lasting result:

Acknowledge:
In which areas of your life have you been expecting results without any real consistent action? What causes you to not take action?

_____

_____

_____

Contemplate:
In what ways has it impacted: you? Write at least one word each in the columns below:

Impact on Myself	
Impact on My Health	
Impact on My Goals	
Impact on My Family	
Impact on My Work	

Take responsibility:

Top three actions that you can take immediately that will bring the significant positive change to this area:

Action Step 1:	
Action Step 2:	
Action Step 3:	

CHAPTER 5

Successful People Do Not Fight Symptoms

"A sum can be put right: but only by going back till you find the error and working it afresh from that point, never by simply going on."

– CS Lewis from The Great Divorce

When you are dealing with an illness, you must get to the root cause rather than fighting with the symptoms.

The attributes that stop you from succeeding are like the symptoms. Not having enough money for your business. Or enough time to get a professional degree that can catapult your career. Or enough time for your family. These are all symptoms.

They may seem like real problems because symptoms are immediate, they are easily visible, and their impact can be felt head-on.

Take for instance the flash floods that caused immeasurable damage in Uttarakhand and Jammu and Kashmir a couple of years ago. Heart-wrenching images of houses collapsing and people being washed away were seen by the entire country. They were some of the most devastating flash floods the country has ever witnessed in the past few centuries.

Although the flash floods were caused by sudden cloudbursts, the real reason was relentless deforestation and greed for money. The mountains have been disrobed. There is nothing to hold the soil. When there is nothing to hold the soil landslides occur and they either block rivers and streams or change their course.

Do you know that most of the living structures that collapsed were built on the mountain sides that had been victims of deforestation? Sadly, such flash floods can occur every year if the root cause is not dealt with and that is deforestation.

Unless more trees are grown on these mountain slopes the soil is always going to remain loose and the loose soil on mountains always causes landslides that trigger massive catastrophes.

If we truly want to put a stop to such devastation's, we have to work at the root cause, the source. We have to plant more trees on the slopes of the mountains and hills. We need to stop building houses where houses are not supposed to be built. We need to deal with the source and not just symptoms.

The same holds true at an individual level.

I was once coaching a leadership executive, who was perceived to be low on empathy. After having spoken with top management and his direct reports the perception was confirmed. During one of our coaching conversations, we dug deeper into the issue. A seemingly small incident from his past had left an imprint in his mind that made him behave the way he did. One day, he came home crying after having lost a match. His dad simply asked him to wash his face and get ready because they had to go somewhere. This incident made him believe that if you love someone or care for them, you don't really need to "show" it. He knew his dad loved him and that was enough for him. Similarly, he cared for people at work, and like his dad he felt he did not need to express it explicitly.

The problem in the first place was not that he didn't care for people, whereas people actually believed that he didn't care. It was just a symptom. Imagine, had I started coaching him to care for people, it would have been a disaster. The guy just needed to "show" that he cared. This became possible only when we traced the symptom back to its source.

So, go to the root cause. Try to look at the source of the problem, not just the symptom. Instead of constantly keeping yourself busy in firefighting, snuff out the source of the fire.

In fact, in medical science too, symptomatic treatment can be very dangerous, because it camouflages the underlying source of the disease and when it's not treated, it becomes fatal for human life.

Dr. Frank Lipman put it beautifully – "When a plant's leaves are turning brown you don't paint the leaves green. You look at the cause of the problem."

You've read the chapter, you can relate to the examples from your own life, now what?

Now, ACT

Acknowledge. **C**ontemplate. **T**ake Action.

And here's what you can do immediately to bring about a powerful lasting result:

Acknowledge:
In which areas of your life are you fighting only the symptoms? Does it scare you to acknowledge the source?

_____

_____

_____

Contemplate:
In what ways has it impacted: you? Write at least one word each in the columns below:

Impact on Myself	
Impact on My Health	
Impact on My Goals	
Impact on My Family	
Impact on My Work	

Take responsibility:

Top three actions that you can take immediately that will bring the significant positive change to this area:

Action Step 1:	
Action Step 2:	
Action Step 3:	

CHAPTER 6

Successful People Are Not Rigid In Their Thinking

"We cannot solve our problems with the same thinking we used when we created them."

– Albert Einstein

It's a misconception that our fundamental thinking never changes. You must have heard often, "What can I do? I am wired that way." Or something like, "the tiger cannot change its stripes."

Many people think that we are born with particular behaviour patterns, and we have to live them our entire lives. The habits that we acquire while growing up, the opinions that we form after observing the world around us, the heuristic responses that our brain develops, we firmly believe in their reality.

It seems they are unchangeable and no matter what we do, we remain who we are. The philosophy that's deeply ingrained in our system is that the 'fuel of our past, drives the motor of our future.'

This thought process belongs to an era when brain science hadn't much evolved. It has now been proven in neuroscience that our brain can be completely rewired. The progress in the field of neuroplasticity has shown that we have the capacity to change our thinking. We have the capacity to not just change our emotional reactions but also change our mind that controls the physical actions.

You might recall that I had mentioned Abhishek Thaware in chapter 2. Abhishek's life story is a perfect example of how changing our emotional and mental abilities results in new physical realities. Yes, it is possible.

Teeth are not made for archery, but Abhishek, re-trained his mind, rewired his brain, and his thinking in such a way that his teeth now perform the action that his hands were supposed to do.

I remember reading this story about an Eagle that beautifully illustrates the same:

An eaglet got separated from its family at birth. It somehow landed at a chicken farm and grew up with tiny little chickens. Eaglet grew up believing it was a chicken too.

One day, this eaglet saw a bird fly over the farm. It was awestruck to see a bird fly like that. It asked its brethren about this magnificent bird. They told the eaglet; it was an eagle. The little eaglet was bemused and said, "wow, it's awesome to be free and flying like that." The chickens said that it was awesome indeed, but chickens can't fly. And that my friends, was the end of it for the little eaglet. It never flew.

There's something I love about stories. Number one, stories have a huge impact on us. Number two, just like life, if you don't like the way it ends; you can choose to have a happy ending... or a new beginning.

So, here's another version of the same story.

A few days after this incident, a young man visited the chicken farm and he saw this eaglet acting and behaving exactly like a chicken. He observed the eaglet closely. It was pecking on the grains along with other chickens. He was extremely curious and asked the farm owner about this peculiar behaviour. The farm owner explained that the eaglet came to this farm as a baby and grew up with these chickens. This bird believes it is a chicken and that's why it acts like that!

The young man was surprised and asked the farmer if it could try to make the bird fly. The farm owner said you could try, but it won't fly. The young man picked the eagle up and dropped it on the other side of the fence, but the eagle did not even make an attempt to fly. The moment it fell on the ground, it went running inside the farm.

He picked the eagle once again and the same thing happened. Every time he tried; the eagle did not fly. Finally, the farm owner told the young man it is not going to fly, it's not an eagle anymore.

The young man believed that it could fly, and it should. He requested the farm owner to give him one last chance. This time, the young man took the eagle on the top of the mountain far away from the farm. And this time he threw the eagle in the air. The moment the eagle found itself falling, it slowly stretched itself physically and spread its wings and began to fly.

This story is very relevant to the context of this chapter. The eagle became a chicken because of the environment it grew in. The eagle had lost its natural ability to fly. Even when the eagle had an inspiration to fly, its surroundings once again did not allow it to soar in the sky. Finally, the eagle altered its reality when the young man threw it from the top of the mountain.

Thinking can be changed. Reality can be altered. You can have a brand-new life. And the point is successful people are not rigid in their thinking.

Think about it. You may have heard of the phrase "When you change the way you look at things, the things you look at change."

The choice is yours.

I'm not talking about changing your DNA. I'm simply saying that if you think you're thinking cannot be changed, think it again: it can be.

Now coming to the moot point of the chapter.

I started with a quote from Albert Einstein. "We cannot solve our problems with the same thinking we used when we created them." Like I mentioned in the previous chapter, unless you deal with the root cause of the problem, the source of the problem, you cannot eliminate the problem. There is no use fighting the symptoms because the symptoms will recur unless their source is treated.

But how do you change the way you think?

How can you control what you think?

Before I get into addressing these nerve wracking questions, here's something you should know. Among all the species existing on our planet, we are the only ones who can think of thinking. French mathematician, scientist, and philosopher René Descartes famously said, "I think, therefore I am," which basically means (aside from the philosophical explanation) we think, and this is what makes us human.

On top of that, we don't just think, we can also think of thinking. For example, if you're feeling angry and frustrated, you can accurately identify the feeling (in most of the cases); for example, you can tell yourself "I feel angry and frustrated."

Let's come back to the questions now. How do you change the way you think? How can you control what you think?

Most of us experience certain thoughts that constantly nag us. So much so that they form a stubborn part of our personality.

More often than not, these thoughts are negative. First, you need to identify that negative thoughts drain you out and stop you from achieving your potential. Second, you must curb the negative feelings and simply switch over to positive ones. It's that simple.

The negative feelings are hugely influenced by the environment, especially these days. You read the newspaper, switch television sets on, and you are bombarded with negativity. Early morning your mind is attacked with news of crime, corruption, murders, accidents, etc.

Here's a snapshot of this morning's newspaper (by the way, it is the same story every morning):

> **Class 9 boy rapes 5-year-old in Noida**
>
> **20 Yemeni civilians reported dead in air strike**
>
> **Actress told father she wants divorce day before killing self**
>
> Blind woman identifies her blind rapist in Ggn court
>
> Caution: A deadly virus is on its way
>
> Abductors drugged, terrorised doctor, say police

We are surrounded by greed, lust and negativity. And these negative influences contribute hugely to making you negatively rigid. You begin to see the world through scratched glasses. When we start believing these thoughts as real, we develop an obstinate incapacity to refuse and to acknowledge another point of view.

Here are a few scratches that spoil your vision and make you rigid in your thought:

- Newspaper and television: There's rarely some positive news in the media these days. Open a newspaper and every headline has the capacity to depress you. Watch some TV program and you see vicious people conspiring against each other. Watch news channels and you are scared out of your wits. Go on social media, you are bound to come across something negative. There's hostility, distrust, grimness all around. The sooner you recognise this fact, the better it will be for you.

- The company you keep. There's a very popular saying in Hindi "Buri Sangat Ka Asar Bura Hee Hota Hai." Negativity of people around you rub off on you and floods you with negative thoughts. And two negatives do not make a positive in this case. This is exactly what happened with the eaglet in the story I shared. The company of chickens made it believe that it's a chicken and cannot fly. What company are you keeping? What kind of conversation do you have with your friends over dinner?

- Your internal dialogue – This is the most important. The sort of conversations that you have with yourself have a great impact on your outlook about the world and the problems that you face. As Mahatma Gandhi said, "You cannot control what other people do to you, but you can always control your reaction."

Let's ponder over the third point a bit more. As I have mentioned already, it is one of the most important sources that make us rigid.

Our thoughts create us, whether we realise it or not. They change the neurons inside our brain. When negative, pessimistic and cynical thoughts are processed inside our brain, it begins to produce toxins.

Everything around you begin to seem dark and dismal. You begin to lose faith in humanity and start distrusting people around you. It breeds sternness in thought and action. Take, for example, the following negative thoughts:

- I always get an unfair deal
- I'm not lucky
- I don't know enough
- I never got an opportunity and I'm never going to get one
- I never got the right guidance
- I'm not as smart as others
- I don't have enough resources or the right kind
- In my heart I know I'm going to fail
- The universe just doesn't want me to succeed

You will be surprised to know that most of these negative thoughts are excuses, really. We use these excuses to justify our shortcomings. We just don't want to move out of our comfort zone, and we hide under the shroud of these excuses.

Do you know that people also get comfortable with their

captor? This is called Stockholm syndrome. Similarly, we get comfortable with our negative feelings and don't want to do away with them. You already know, the moment you drop these negative thoughts, you will be left with nothing to hide behind. We become rigid without even realising it. We fall in love with our captors, our negative beliefs, our negative feelings.

So, how do you change your thinking?

Big changes can be made with the help of a mentor, a guide or a confidant who understands you, doesn't judge you, and who can nudge you in the right direction. I've had the opportunity to help hundreds and thousands of people get rid of their negative thoughts and become fluid, receptive, a little less rigid may be; to bring about great changes in their lives.

But even on your own, you can do this. Here's a little secret that's deceptively simple, and if you practise it, you can get rid of it. Are you ready? Here's what you gotta do – simply drop these thoughts.

It is as simple as replacing the negative thoughts with the positive ones. For example:

So, what if life is difficult? I am resilient.

So, what if I don't know enough? Every new day is a learning opportunity.

I'm going to create my own opportunities for myself. If I never got the right guidance, I'm going to seek it now. I'm smart and that's why I am where I am, and I'm going to make myself smarter. People are able to achieve much with zero resources, I still have many. Without trying, how can I know whether I'm going to succeed or fail and if there is no sure shot way of knowing it, why not bet on succeeding? The hell with the crabs that pull me down, if I decide to succeed, I WILL succeed.

I totally understand if you think it is easier said than done, but you can definitely start with small things and before you know, you will realise that your whole thinking is changed.

Remember, our thoughts become our words, and our words create our world.

– Magan Kalra

You've read the chapter, you can relate to the examples from your own life, now what?

Now, ACT

Acknowledge. **C**ontemplate. **T**ake Action.

And here's what you can do immediately to bring about a powerful lasting result:

Acknowledge:
Are you being rigid in any area of your life or with anybody? What makes your thinking rigid?

_____

_____

_____

Contemplate:
In what ways has it impacted: you? Write at least one word each in the columns below:

Impact on Myself	
Impact on My Health	
Impact on My Goals	
Impact on My Family	
Impact on My Work	

Take responsibility:

Top three actions that you can take immediately that will bring the significant positive change to this area:

Action Step 1:	
Action Step 2:	
Action Step 3:	

BONUS CHAPTER

7

Successful People Do Not Get Disillusioned By The Comfort Of Smart Work

"Hard work without talent is a shame, but talent without hard work is a tragedy."

~ Robert Half

Today the internet is flooded with "work smarter" blog posts and articles that look down upon people who work hard and put in extra hours and prompt you to look up to people who work smart, reduce their work hours, and consequently, achieve more.

Ironically mobile app developers work hard to trick you into believing that smart work is more important than working hard. In fact, so much so, it has convinced an entire generation that hard work is not meant for smart people and this gets validated again and again when I interview younger people who have just started their careers and in some cases have not even started their careers, their mantra has become smart work instead of hard work. Imagine a whole generation hates the idea of working hard.

So much phobia has been created around working hard and so much hype has been created around working smart that sometimes even the thought of having to work harder than the guy sitting next to you makes you feel like a loser. If you are working harder, you begin to feel that there is something wrong with you.

Guess what? All those productivity experts are burning the night oil churning out advice for you that you shouldn't be burning the night oil. The life coaches that advise you to work smarter rather than harder are working hard at creating such "educational material" for which then, they charge a premium.

They work hard at convincing you not to work hard.

What's the difference between working harder and working smarter?

There isn't, actually. Needlessly, an entire industry has been created advising people how they can avoid working hard by working smart.

Now, in the age of computers, laptops and convertible tablets, I'm not suggesting that I'm writing this e-book on a sheet of paper that was pulped and matted in 1783 with a quill that was carved in the same year. That would be dumb, no? Unless I'm trying to prove something.

Needless toiling is always wasteful. There is no need to reinvent the wheel. There is no need to rediscover the fire. There is no need to write a piece of code if that piece of code, in its most efficient form, already exists, and is available to you. If I'm using a word processor to write this, I'm not using a word processor that I got exclusively built to write this. I bought a word processor in a matter of a few seconds.

Making notes when studying instead of trying to memorize the entire book is smart work. Using cue cards to memorize stuff is smart work. Using public transport to save fuel or to avoid getting stuck in traffic is smart work. Obtaining code libraries from GitHub is a smarter decision compared to building all the libraries yourself.

There is no problem in working smarter. Then what's the problem?

The strong desire to work smart becomes a problem when you seek smarter ways to work, to avoid working hard. This way, you start resenting hard work. Smart ways of doing work should be sought so that you do more work, not to do less work.

If you want to succeed in life, develop a habit of working hard; working smart will automatically become part of the game because the more you work, the smarter you get. Fall in love with working hard. Feel proud of it. Feel blessed that you can work hard.

Some wise man rightly said, "Don't wish it were easier. Wish you were better."

Prolonged hard work is followed by long lasting success. Some people succeed by fluke. Most don't.

Of course, weird and seemingly unfair things happen in this world, and you come across people who seem to have all the luck in the world with little or no work. Some people can manipulate their way to success.

How many world-renowned and successful people can you count who are extremely successful or enjoy a powerful social position and you believe that they haven't earned their success. How many? One? Two? Three? And no, I'm not talking about politicians like Rahul Gandhi, Justin Trudeau or even Donald Trump.

What about Amitabh Bachchan? Sachin Tendulkar? Saina Nehwal? Mark Zuckerberg? Bill Gates? Mukesh Ambani? Narendra Modi?

"Nothing in this world is achieved without pain, hard work, sweat, blood and tears, the sooner we reconcile this fact the better; the sooner we start to act on it even better!" Amitabh Bachchan famously wrote this on his blog. Even during his heydays, he was one of the first to arrive on the sets and when his co-stars didn't come prepared even for their own dialogues, he would know dialogues of every character in the script.

They call him God. But was Sachin Tendulkar born a God? Cricket experts say that Sachin Tendulkar and Vinod Kambli had the same potential and in fact, in the beginning, Kambli showed more potential than Tendulkar? Sachin Tendulkar started playing international cricket when he was 16 and he retired after almost 25 years. How many players have played for so many years? Only his hard work and dedication kept him so fit and focused. His roommate, Suru Nayak, once told in a newspaper interview that even as a 14-year-old, during cricket camps, when other boys slept, Tendulkar would practice his shots at night.

Bill Gates in his book claimed that after starting Microsoft, he took his first break after seven years. Author Walter Isaacson wrote in a 2013 issue of the Harvard Gazette: "In the wee hours of the morning, Gates would sometimes fall asleep at the terminal. He'd be in the middle of a line of code when he'd gradually tilt forward until his nose touched the keyboard. After dozing an hour or two, he'd open his eyes, squint at the screen, blink twice, and resume precisely where he'd left off-a prodigious feat of concentration."

Apple CEO Tim Cook is known to send emails to his employees at 4:30 in the morning. He is the first in the office and the last to leave.

In the early days of Amazon. com, Jeff Bezos used to work for 12 hours a day, seven days a week. Staying up until 3 a.m. to make sure that all the books were being shipped on time, was a norm. In fact, even when he was in school, his capacity to work extremely hard was quite well-known. Once, he declared in high school that he was going to be that year's valedictorian. Everybody else gave up because they knew that they were competing for second place.

Steve Jobs repeatedly said in his speeches that most of the successful entrepreneurs he had met in his life had one single common trait – perseverance(ability to work hard no matter what).

Both Venus and Serena Williams started practicing at 6 a.m. even when they were 7 and 8 years old.

Michael Jordan used to spend his off-season taking hundreds of jump shots every day.

When Marissa Mayer worked at Google, pulling all-nighters was a routine for her. No wonder, as Yahoo CEO, even when the individual assets of the company were being auctioned off, she took home $60 million as a severance package!

Indira Nooyi, Pepsi CEO, worked as a receptionist from midnight to 5 a.m. while pursuing her Master's degree at Yale. Even today her day starts at 4 a.m.

SpaceX and Tesla CEO Elon Musk says that if the others are putting in 40 hours a week, you need to put in 80-100 hours, and this is how he works.

Malcom Gladwell in his book Outliers says that studies have found that to become a world-class performer, in any field, takes 10,000 hours of practice. You want to be a world-class musician? Practice for 10,000 hours. You want to be a world-class player? Practice for 10,000 hours. Want to be a world-class doctor? Study medicine and treat patients for 10,000 hours.

The rule is not written in stone, but it is the average time a world-class performer takes to master his or her skill.

The more you read about success and successful people, the more you discover that often, "overnight success" takes decades of toiling and hard work.

In fact this reminds me of an ad by TATA for their passenger car business, it was a full page ad in the newspaper with Lionel Messi's picture and the text read, it took me 17 years and 114 days to be an overnight success.

I'm not saying that working smart is bad. As I established earlier, working smart doesn't mean working less, it simply means working better so that you can work more.

Suppose you have found a way to write a piece of code in 30 minutes and the other programmers in your company take two hours to write the same piece of code. You quickly complete your work, feel good about it, and then while away the remaining time on unproductive activities. You don't utilise the extra one-and-a-half hours that you have got learning new programming techniques or learning a new language. After a while, you begin to stagnate.

The initial cool factor is gone. People begin to take for granted the fact that you can code really fast. Although you are still working smarter, it's no big deal.

If you want to grow, then you put the extra time you have got (by working smarter) by honing your skill, learning another language, or even developing managerial skills so that instead of a coder, you can become a project manager, if that interests you.

On an average, an individual works for 35 hours every week. Officially, it is 40 hours – if you have a 9-to-5 job then you are supposedly working for 40 hours. Basically, everybody is working this much, and if you were too, what is special about you?

Almost all self-made millionaires (I'm not talking about jackpot winners) in America, or even all over the world, on an average work 59 hours every week, that's 19 hours more than an average person does. Many of them, especially at the start of their careers or business ventures, put in on an average 70-80 hours every week. They are the first ones to enter the office and the last ones to leave.

Having said that, there is a big difference between people who are always "busy" and people who really work.

Some people may appear to be busy all the time, working all the time, while achieving very little. They may go to the office early but then they spend most of the time near the water cooler gossiping. Or chatting on their phones. Then they leave late because they can't complete their work on time. These are procrastinators. They work in spurts, but most of the time, they're simply whiling away their time despite sitting in the cubicle longer than the others. They are neither good for themselves, nor for others.

When you are working, work.

How to inculcate a habit of hard work?

Don't beat yourself up by thinking that you haven't got what other successful people have got – the ability to walk the extra mile.

A good thing about habits is people are not born with habits. A habit is all about doing something so regularly that it becomes second nature. In the beginning, it may take an effort but as you do it every day, it becomes a habit. The same goes for the habit of working hard. Listed below are a few things you can do to develop a habit of working hard:

Have a clear goal in mind.

It is difficult to work hard if you don't know exactly what you are trying to achieve. When you have a clearly-defined goal, you can put in more effort because you have a sense of purpose and when you have a sense of purpose, your body produces adrenaline that helps you to push hard.

Work on smaller goals.

When climbing a mountain, focus on your next step, not the

summit. If bigger goals intimidate you and stop you from working hard, divide your bigger goals into smaller goals.

Suppose you want to make a career switch. What are the things you will need for that switch? Some educational qualification? Some skill? Networking?

Skill let's suppose. Make a list of things you want to learn. Forget about the bigger goal for the time being. Your only goal right now is acquiring that skill.

Create realistic deadlines. Allocate time of the day. Practice the skill. Practice in small chunks. Give yourself multiple scopes to err.

Even when you don't see progress, remember one thing: if you practiced yesterday, if you practice today, whether you realize it or not, you will be better tomorrow than you were the day before yesterday.

Develop a system to measure your time. You will be amazed to know how much time you actually spend working when you start tracking your time. When you track your time, you become cautious.

For example, if you think every morning, you start working

(actual work) at 9:30, set a timer on your phone (or whatever device you prefer), and immediately stop the timer the moment you think you are doing something else. Then start the timer when you resume. By the end of your schedule, just count the number of hours you actually put in doing real work. Just sitting in front of your computer or laptop doesn't count, and I hope you know that. In fact, I did the same and I was astonished and happy. Astonished because I realised that I was wasting a lot of my time on trivia. And I was happy because now I know that I can plan better and be more efficient i.e., Smarter. Practice mindfulness and focus on one thing at a time because multitasking is a myth.

This will help you if you easily get distracted. In the hubbub of life, it is difficult to get into the ideal situation. There are always going to be distractions. People are always going to demand your attention. You either complain, make an excuse and then give up, or you learn to focus amidst distractions.

Increase your time in small steps. If you are used to working for 6 hours every day you won't suddenly start working for 12. It will take time.

First, make sure that those 6 hours you spend working are actually spent working. Then start taking small steps of 30 minutes. You don't need to increment every day. Work with these extra 30 minutes for a couple of weeks and see how you feel. If you're comfortable, start putting in 30 minutes more.

No matter what you do, how you do, how much and how hard you work, you are the judge. It is very important that you are totally sincere with yourself. The desire to work hard has to come from within. If you are fine with it, make yourself more accountable by sharing your plans with another person and ask the other person to hold you accountable by sharing your plans with another person and also ask the other person to hold you accountable. Unfortunately, though, as human beings when we are held accountable, most of us don't like it.

You need clarity. You need desire. In the beginning, you also need some sort of mechanism to track your performance.

Find smart ways of working, not to reduce your work, but to create more time to work more.

If there's one guaranteed way to get lucky, then that way is hard work. Period.

-Magan Kalra

You've read the chapter, you can relate to the examples from your own life, now what?

Now, ACT

Acknowledge. **C**ontemplate. **T**ake Action.

And here's what you can do immediately to bring about a powerful lasting result:

Acknowledge:
Which areas of your life have you not been getting real results? Have you really, and I mean REALLY worked hard or have you only been thinking hard? What are you willing to do now?

_____

_____

_____

Contemplate:
In what ways has it impacted: you? Write at least one word each in the columns below:

Impact on Myself	
Impact on My Health	
Impact on My Goals	
Impact on My Family	
Impact on My Work	

Take responsibility:

Top three actions that you can take immediately that will bring the significant positive change to this area:

Action Step 1:	
Action Step 2:	
Action Step 3:	

Bonus Chapter

8

Successful People Do Not Give up

"Circumstances do not make the man, they merely reveal him to himself."

– Epictetus, a Greek Stoic philosopher.

In the above-mentioned quote, what do you understand by "not giving up?"

Is this phrase associated with a mythical hero (or a film hero) who doesn't give up under extremely trying and seemingly insurmountable circumstances and then eventually, with persistence, courage and love, triumphs?

The problem with popular literature, folklore and cinema is that it feeds into your mind that only great heroes know how to persist. They are conditioned to persist. They are born to persist. Not normal folks.

Normal folks easily give up. We are conditioned to believe that we are merely toys in the hands of fate or the proverbial "Almighty." Somehow, we disillusion ourselves into believing that the ideas of controlling your fate and carving our own destiny are merely philosophical ideas.

Epictetus, one of the greatest Greek philosophers, differed. He would know. He was a slave. He was banished from his own city. Born more than 2000 years ago, he still wields influence among those who genuinely want to understand how to succeed in life, despite life.

He invited people to consider that when they say that they have no control over what happens to them is a mere excuse for them not wanting to take responsibility for their own lives.

Though he believed that all external events are beyond our control. There is an earthquake, you cannot control it. The market suddenly crashes, no control. The war breaks out in the continent and your business suffers, no control. Someone (or you) falls sick in the family and all your savings are gone within a couple of weeks. Your company loses a few contracts, and you lose your job. No control.

Epictetus said that although you may have no control over what life throws at you, you have total control over how you react or how you respond.

There's a very popular phrase. "When life gives you lemons, make a lemonade." Yet most of us keep blaming luck and circumstances.

Another wise person has said: "When life throws stones at me, I make them into steppingstones."

When people say that they can control their destiny and they are responsible for their own actions, what it means is it is they who decide how they are going to react to adversities. One needs to internalize this philosophy, Epictetus often affirmed to his doting disciples.

How can you positively take on adversities if you are conditioned to believe that you are not in control and you need luck to succeed?

Conditioning is a double-edged phenomenon. It can turn you into a victim and it can also turn you into a champion.

But a great thing about conditioning is that you can develop it. It is a misconception that we are born with a predetermined attitude or way of thinking. This is not so. We can change our way of thinking. If our brain is conditioned in a certain manner, with practice and desire we can recondition it, and that's exactly what I established in previous chapters too.

Mental conditioning is like physical training. Why do you think athletes seem to have supernatural strength? Are they born with that strength?

No, they are just like normal human beings. The difference is, when they feel tired, they don't give up. In fact, they believe that the real training starts when they are tired. Normal folks rest when they get tired, champions get going when they are tired.

Have you heard Arunima Sinha's story? She is the first amputee to climb Mount Everest in the world. Although, the very fact that she not only decided to conquer the highest peak in the world, but actually did it, makes her a great champion, but do you know what makes her a greater champion? Her ability to fight back when people would have just given up on life.

Before losing her leg, she was a national level volleyball player. During a scuffle with some train robbers in 2011, she was pushed out of the moving train by the robbers. She fell on the parallel rail track and couldn't move despite seeing another train that eventually ran over her leg.

Losing a limb, to any person, would seem like the end of the road, but you can very well imagine what she must have gone through, being a sports person of national level. Not just her sports career was over, she was rendered physically disabled for the rest of her life.

But she was not conditioned to wallow in self-pity. While she was having her treatment at All India Institute of Medical

Sciences, there itself she resolved to climb Mount Everest. As soon as she started walking with a prosthetic leg, she contacted Bachendri Pal, the first Indian woman to climb Mount Everest. The rest is history.

The attack of robbers, the losing of a limb, these things were not in her control. How she reacted, was.

While lying in the hospital bed itself, she decided that although her life seemed to have taken a turn for the worse, instead of playing a victim, she was going to play a hero. She was destined to do something great. Her destination didn't change. Just the route changed.

Seems like stuff epics are made of. Not necessarily. She is of the same flesh and blood you are. It is just a matter of attitude.

And the great thing is, if somehow you have conditioned yourself into believing that you don't have such an attitude, you can train yourself to build and sustain such an attitude.

It is not very difficult. You don't even have to face monumental problems to build your moral and attitudinal strength. You just need a strategy and a little bit of practice.

Listed below are a few suggestions you can incorporate in

your daily life that will definitely help you take control of your life no matter what circumstances are around you.

When you accept that life is unpredictable and chaotic, and all sorts of bad things happen to all sorts of people, you are at peace. You know that difficulties come in life, and they are a natural part of life. After all, what makes a good story-an intent, an obstacle and the process of overcoming the obstacles. From Ramayana to Mahabharata, and from Titanic to Harry Potter, it's about an intent, an obstacle and the process of overcoming the obstacles.

You can lose your job. Millions of people before you have. You can fall sick. Millions of people fall sick every day. You can meet with an accident. According to government data, one serious road accident happens in the country every minute and 16 people die on Indian roads every hour.

Of course, reading about these unfortunate occurrences and actually going through them is a totally different thing, but what I mean to say is, they are very much a part-and-parcel of the world we live in. Once you accept this, you don't feel that you are being singled out by a great power or destiny.

IF YOU WANT TO MAKE POSITIVE CHANGES IN YOUR LIFE, START EMBRACING CHANGE.

Do you know what we fear and consequently, try to avoid the most? Change.

We are creatures of habit. When we lose a job, aside from the fact that the most important source of income has been suddenly snatched away, we also resent the sudden change. Suddenly you won't be going to the same office. Suddenly you won't be interacting with the same people. Suddenly you won't be taking the same routes.

Someone falls sick. Your routine has suddenly changed. Whether interesting or boring, the everyday tasks can no longer be performed. Your brain is alarmed that you are not able to indulge in activities you indulge in every day.

So, while you have the luxury to take small steps, start accepting change in your life by proactively introducing small changes.

Drink tea in a different cup. Take a different route when going to the office. Wear something you normally don't wear (no, I'm not suggesting borrowing a sari from your wife). Greet someone you don't like and mean it. Try a new dish. Stretch your intellectual boundaries and read a book you find difficult to understand. Skip an episode on TV and instead, go for a walk.

These activities and actions may seem irrelevant, but gradually, your brain begins to accept change naturally, and when the time comes, when you really need to adapt quickly, your brain, and even your body, will be ready.

Have a clear idea of what you want to achieve in life, and more importantly, why?

Most of the time we are just stumbling into various phases in life. When was the last time you sat for a couple of hours and thought about what exactly you want to do in life? Really sit somewhere with a notepad and pen and write down your thoughts? Or sit with someone and talk about what you want to achieve, why you want to achieve it, and how you plan to achieve it?

How can you have a strong desire to achieve something if you haven't clearly thought of what you want to achieve?

Have clearly-defined goals and have a purpose for those goals. Don't just randomly decide what you want to achieve just because everybody around you wants to achieve that.

You might have seen a lot of people start doing things today just because someone else is doing it or perhaps because it sounds cool. For example, I see a lot of youngsters leaving their jobs or not being focused on one because they think "start-up" is cool, and then to justify their stupidity they share stories of rich people in terms of how they left their education and are millionaires or billionaires today, it saddens me to see that they totally get the point wrong. Most of us don't realise that we do this out of social pressure and psychology even has a term for it, it's called Social Proof, and just as peer pressure is for teens, similarly social proof is for adults. Just because most of your friends and colleagues have the iPhone doesn't mean you need to have it too, but we don't get it and have all the reasons to justify our decision to buy the phone. You see your connections on social media enjoying a vacation in Goa or maybe some exotic location out of the country, it doesn't mean you too need to have the same vacation, but most tend to give into the social proof.

Arunima wasn't just stuck up on the idea of becoming a volleyball champion. Retrospectively, being a volleyball player was just a means to an end. What she was striving for was doing something great, giving her best no matter what she did. If it wasn't volleyball, it was mountaineering, and if it was mountaineering, why not climb the biggest rock in the world? That was her driving force, to do something big. If it weren't mountaineering, it would have been something else. Having a clear idea of what you want to do and why you want to do it, gives you the ability to persist.

Do you think you don't have it in you? Don't beat yourself up. If you don't fear something and you, do it, it's no big deal. The big deal is, you fear something, but you conquer your fear and do it anyway. That is a true act of bravery.

Similarly, if you are persistent just by nature, no big deal. But, if you inculcate this habit of persisting from scratch, now, that will be true achievement, and you will be more prone to achieving success in your life.

Decide to do something, something good, but may be insignificant. For example, not letting clutter accumulate in your room for two weeks. Or, if you have a sweet tooth, not eating any sweets for a week. Or, not watching TV for a week and reading a book instead, or indulging in an activity that makes you smarter, like solving puzzles or trying out crosswords.

READ ABOUT PEOPLE WHO HAVE STRUGGLED AND SUCCEEDED

Reading biographies, anecdotes and articles about successful people isn't always about motivation and pep talk. These stories hold great insights into how this world works, and how different people take decisions under different circumstances.

Although everyone is unique, thousands of people have gone through the same problems you are facing now. It's just that because you are facing them, you think that you are the only one to face them.

There are numerous books written on people (either by themselves or their biographers) who overcame monumental difficulties and achieved what they wanted to achieve. Even when they couldn't get what they wanted, they used their new circumstances to create or find new opportunities for themselves. By reading about them, you can find solutions that you couldn't have found around you or within yourself. Even if you don't find a solution, you no longer feel alone. You feel a sense of affinity towards those people who have gone through similar situations.

The best time to prepare yourself is when there is no need to prepare. Start being persistent from today itself. Take baby steps if you want or just plunge into the pool of persistence headfirst – whatever is your style. The change that you begin to experience will be amazing, even beyond your imagination. You will be surprised to discover your ability to persist. Suddenly, you will be unstoppable.

Most challenges in life that may appear to be mountains are mere speed breakers.

-Magan Kalra

You've read the chapter, you can relate to the examples from your own life, now what?

Now, ACT

Acknowledge. **C**ontemplate. **T**ake Action.

And here's what you can do immediately to bring about a powerful lasting result:

Acknowledge:
Where all in your life and on who all have you given up? What can you do differently now? What actions would make the biggest difference to you?

_____

_____

_____

Contemplate:
In what ways has it impacted: you? Write at least one word each in the columns below:

Impact on Myself	
Impact on My Health	
Impact on My Goals	
Impact on My Family	
Impact on My Work	

Take responsibility:

Top three actions that you can take immediately that will bring the significant positive change to this area:

Action Step 1:	
Action Step 2:	
Action Step 3:	

BLOG

1

8 Great Words Of Wisdom From Movies

by Magan Kalra

Access Magan's blogs online:
www.magankalra.com

Movies are not only an extraordinary form of entertainment but also a great source of learning just as most stories are. I have put together some of my favorites, not all though, else this blog would be titled as "100 Great Words of Wisdom from Movies" instead of 8. Listed below are 8 great words of wisdom from iconic as well as lesser-known movies. Usually what you learn from these quotes depends on you but there is timeless wisdom in these quotes.

1. **"If you're good at something, never do it for free."**
This is from Batman, Joker said this, and if You are someone who has ever had a dilemma whether to charge for your services or not, your dilemma should end here. In particular this is very apt in the business world and from a branding and positioning perspective too.

2. **"With great power comes great responsibility."**
No prize for guessing this one, one of my all time favorites. In fact, when you look at it from a leadership perspective it kind of clears the smog for you, because leadership isn't only about titles, it's about taking complete responsibility for your business and your people.

3. "Do or do not. There is no try."

This is one of the most quoted quotes from Star Wars, spoken by Yoda, the Jedi Master full of cosmic wisdom. It simply means either you are committed, or you are not. When you want to do something don't say that I may or may not succeed. At the decision and conviction level either you do it or you don't do it. This quote from Star Wars teaches you to take firm decisions and then to stick to those decisions.

4. Something similar from the original Karate kid.

When Miyagi asks Daniel whether he is ready to learn or not Daniel says, "I guess so." Miyagi uses the example of walking on the road. Walk on the right side safe, walk on the left side safe, walk in the middle, you get squished just like a grape.

5. "I figure life's a gift and I don't intend on wasting it.

You don't know what hand you're gonna get dealt next. You learn to take life as it comes at you. . . to make each day count." Jack Dawson, the character played by Leonardo Di Caprio in the Titanic says this. We often come across the phrase that life is a gift, but do we ever take it seriously? We don't even realize that we are breathing constantly but let the ability to breathe be taken away even for a few seconds and it can turn into a matter of life and death. So, every breath that you take, is another chance for you to live. Whether you want to do something with your life or you don't is totally up to you, but if you want to do something then every day is a gift. Make the most of it. Life is full of unpredictable twists and turns. The time and the opportunities that you have right now with you may not be there tomorrow. Make full use of them.

6. **"Great men are not born great, they grow great."**

By Mario Puzo in The Godfather.

This is the theme of many of my workshops and seminars too. Nobody is born great. Our actions to circumstances make us great. It's how we take decisions and then stick to them. It's how we stick to our values. It's how we react or choose to react when confronted with adversity and enticement. Greatness is not inherent although certain characteristics might be. Greatness can always be nurtured if you have the desire to be great.

7. **"Don't ever let someone tell you that you can't do something. Not even me.**

You got a dream, you gotta protect it. When people can't do something themselves, they're gonna tell you that you can't do it. You want something, go get it. Period."

-Will Smith (The Pursuit of Happiness)

You can't even begin to imagine how lucky you are if you have a dream? Most people when asked about their dreams draw a blank. Very few people have a dream or think of having a dream, cause most human beings are going through motions. In fact I've met a lot of people who laughed at me when I shared my dream with them of becoming a top speaker, the best trainer, an author, and in times like these you got to remember these words of wisdom.

8. **Another one from Karate Kid, "There's no such thing as a bad student, only bad teacher."**

-So powerful, completely changes the perspective on how we look at students.

In fact, I relate so powerfully with this that I have made it a tagline for one of my signature Train the Trainer programs, and when trainers come to me and tell me that these set of participants weren't good, I tell them exactly this. Recently there was a Bollywood movie called Hichki on the similar subject with similar dialogue.

BLOG

2

(Right) Practice Makes A (Wo)man Perfect

by Magan Kalra

Access Magan's blogs online:
www.magankalra.com

"My secret is practice."

~ David Beckham

I was inspired to write this blog when both Jonty Rhodes and were invited to an annual leadership convention, and we were both to speak to a group of over hundred people. I was to deliver a piece on leadership and Jonty was to share his experience as a coach and a sports person.

Jonty started his speech by saying "practice doesn't make perfect, it's the 'right' practice that makes you perfect." We both had a great time delivering our speeches, and that is when I had the inspiration of writing this blog.

So, what is practice?

In layman's terms, practice means doing something repeatedly unless it becomes a reflex action. You get so used to doing that thing that when it comes the time to do it at a competitive level or at a professional level, you can do it without thinking.

In the physical sense, practice builds you the needed muscles. For example, a boxer punches the punching bag thousands of times daily. It builds those muscles in his arms, shoulders, and chest so that when he has to punch his opponent, the muscles are already used to punching with great force.

There is an old saying that "practice makes a man perfect." Now, perfection may have different meanings for different people, what this statement means is, practice continuously improves you. If you repeatedly do the same thing, two things happen: you keep on improving, one, and two, it trains your subconscious.

Training your subconscious is very important. If your subconscious is not trained to perform a particular task, you have to make a conscious effort and when you make a conscious effort, more physical and mental resources are used causing delays and performance lag.

But practice only pays dividends if you do the right practice. Athletes can injure themselves if they practice wrongly. Similarly, if you practice a wrong tactic, you are going to get different results. It's like, there's a famous saying, "boye ped babool ka to aam kahan se hoye?"– if you sow a thorny bush, how do you expect to reap mangoes? No matter how hard you work on that bush, no matter how dedicated you are, ultimately it is going to give you thorns. This is why it is said, "All practice takes hard work but not all-hard work is practice."

Blog 2: (Right) Practice Makes A (Wo)man Perfect

Some people confuse hard work with practice. Hard work can be anything. Taking care of the sick can be hard work. Tending your lawn can be hard work.

Digging a well can be hard work. When you combine this hard work with refining the movements of your body and mind, improvising on a single task so that you perform it elegantly, effortlessly and strongly, and you do it better than any other person, it becomes practice.

Hitting a football 1000 times every day towards the goal post is practice. Using newly-learnt vocabulary to write better is practice. Creating software applications using a programming language is practice. All these activities also require hard work.

What about being a cab driver? You are driving around people all the time. Does that make you a better driver?

It depends on what you want to achieve with your driving skill of driving. If driving is your passion, if you want to make your passengers happy, if you want to make their journeys memorable, then of course, you can practice how to maneuver through traffic jams, you can practice how to avoid potholes and jerks and you can learn new routes to help your passengers save money.

When you use hard work to improve yourself it's practice, otherwise it's simply hard work. Listed below are a few attributes that differentiate practice from hard work:

Recognize a challenge

There is something that you want to improve and then you start improving it through practice. If you want to sing well, you practice the ragas and stretch your vocal chords every day, for months and for years. If you want to be a successful surgeon, you practice on animals (or through computer simulation) or you practice on smaller surgeries. If you want to participate in a marathon, you run every day and then gradually you increase the distance that you cover. You have a challenge in front of you and then to meet that challenge, you repeatedly start doing an activity that will help you eventually meet the challenge.

Define the scope

You cannot work on all the aspects of your skill at one time. You have to decide what you want to improve and then you focus on improving it. If you hop from one practice to another, although you may eventually succeed in doing what you want to do, it will take a lot more effort and a lot more time.

Commit your time

Practice is going to take some time. Although it depends on the sort of challenge you are trying to meet, some forms of practices require a daily schedule, and some don't. When famous footballers skip a practice session it becomes news. When you seriously want to practice, time commitment is of paramount importance.

Use the right tools while practicing

The tools that you use while practicing is as important as the time and effort that you put in. For example, when you are practicing programming, you have to choose your preferred programming language. When you are practicing writing, you need to choose your preferred writing tool, whether you write using a processor, a simple text editor or even the age-old notebook and pen. Make sure that the tools that you use compliment your practice rather than causing you mental and physical harm.

Seek coaching and guidance whenever needed

In order to do the right practice, sometimes you need guidance. Such guidance can only be obtained from a coach, from a trainer, from a guru, or even from study material. The right guru or the right coach can keep you from harming yourself or spending your precious time on unfruitful activities.

Finally, passion and practice go together. Without passion, although you can start practicing, you can't go on practicing. Passion keeps you going on no matter how hard the going gets.

Are you practicing? Are you trying to perfect an art or a skill? What techniques do you follow? How do you make sure that you practice every day without getting discouraged? Do share your thoughts with other readers.

BLOG

3

10 Habits of Successful Entrepreneurs

by Magan Kalra

Access Magan's blogs online:
www.magankalra.com

> "We are what we repeatedly do. Excellence, then, is not an act but a habit."
>
> ~ Aristotle

How do people become successful entrepreneurs? Some may say that they're lucky, but it isn't just luck. Although sometimes luck or "Co-incidents" may play a role, eventually, it's the array of hidden qualities that make entrepreneurs successful.

Besides, what's luck? The wise ones say that luck is "when opportunity meets preparation." This means even luck won't help you if you are not prepared to take advantage of your "lucky" moment.

So, if it isn't plain luck, what makes some entrepreneurs successful? The successful entrepreneurs have these 10 habits or traits.

Successful entrepreneurs value their time.

"Time is money," may sound like a cliché, but what it actually means is that your time is valuable. Successful entrepreneurs know how to value their time. They don't waste their time in unfruitful activities. When people are having casual conversations around the water cooler or checking Facebook updates, successful entrepreneurs are strenuously working on their business ideas or laying the building blocks of their success.

Successful entrepreneurs know how to prioritize.

If you want to be a successful entrepreneur, it is very important that you learn to prioritize your activities. Do you want to attend a party or attend a business call? Do you want to work on your business project, or do you want to complete the 6th season of The Game of Thrones?

You can set priorities when you have a clear idea of what you want to achieve and whether the current task helps you achieve that or not. If it doesn't, the current task does not belong to your priority list.

Successful entrepreneurs take responsibility of their actions.

When you take responsibility for your actions you feel empowered. If you take the responsibility, you know that whatever happens in your life, another individual or some outer circumstance isn't responsible (of course you can't be responsible for an earthquake or an asteroid hitting the Earth) and it is simply cause and effect. Bhagvat Gita says it's karma:

what you send out to the universe comes back to you. Successful entrepreneurs never blame others.

Successful entrepreneurs readily take risks.

Normally, what does a risk mean? Taking a risk means doing something that is unknown, something that is new, something of which the outcome is not known. But, this is how new business ideas take shape – you do something that no one else has done before. When you do something new, you don't know whether it is going to work or not; this is what taking a risk is. Things don't always work, and that is fine. Successful entrepreneurs take risks and are ready to face the consequences because they know that if they succeed, they're going to get great rewards.

Successful entrepreneurs know when to delegate.

If you are constantly being bogged down by day-to-day business operations, you are not going to get time to expand your business. Successful entrepreneurs know when to delegate. A single person is not supposed to do everything even if he can do everything. Just because you can handle phone calls from your customers doesn't mean that you spend all your time handling phone calls because this is something that can easily be delegated to someone else while you focus on growing your business. If the work you're doing right now can be done by someone else, let it be done by someone else.

Successful entrepreneurs know when to move on.

It isn't necessary that everything works. Sometimes no matter how hard you work, no matter how innovative your idea is, it just doesn't work. Either its time hasn't come yet or there is simply no need for it. Successful entrepreneurs know when to move on when things don't work. They don't get stuck. They understand that failure is as integral a part of growing as an entrepreneur as success. Faced with failure, successful entrepreneurs know when to persist and when to move on.

Successful entrepreneurs invest in themselves.

Successful entrepreneurs constantly evolve. They are always learning. They are always reading books, articles, attending seminars and interacting with learned people. No matter at what stage they are, they know that their knowledge and wisdom is going to grow obsolete with time and they need to update themselves.

Investing in oneself doesn't just mean acquiring new intellectual skills. It also means investing in good health. It also means investing in your family, in relationships, in society, in building a network, and in other good things in life.

Successful entrepreneurs are good networkers.

Business success doesn't manifest in isolation. You have to work with people. Whether you work freelance or you have a complete enterprise under you, you're going to need people, you're going to need resource persons, and you're going to need evangelists – people who can help you grow your business by word of mouth.

Successful entrepreneurs are good at networking. They are good with people. They are good with people-to-people contacts.

Networking doesn't just mean getting to know people that can get you business. Networking also means creating goodwill among the people who know you.

Successful entrepreneurs develop strong habits.

One of the most important traits of successful entrepreneurs is that they develop very strong habits. Whether it is getting up very early in the morning, doing regular reading and studying, doing exercise, eating and avoiding certain foods or wearing certain clothes, all successful entrepreneurs develop habits that keep them focused and charged up. And they tenaciously cling onto their habits because I know that once they begin to get lenient with them, it is a sure shot way downwards.

Successful entrepreneurs keep negativity away.

Negativity is a big energy drainer. Negativity fills you with pacifism and blocks your creativity. You must have experienced yourself that when you are full of negative thoughts (envy, anger, dejection, frustration) your spirits are sapped of energy. Sometimes you don't even feel like moving and forget about building your business. The problem with negativity is once you allow it to settle down within your subconscious mind, you don't realise when it becomes a permanent resident.

It's not those successful entrepreneurs are immune to negativity. It's just that they know how to handle it and how to get rid of it. You can develop certain rituals that give you a better perspective the moment you feel that the dark clouds of negativity are beginning to hover above you.

> *"Genius is 1% inspiration, 99% perspiration."*
>
> *~ Thomas Alva Edison.*

In the end, successful entrepreneurs are hard-working. They know the importance of hard work and persistence. They don't give up easily no matter how hard a situation is. Thomas Edison also said "I have not failed. I have just found 10,000 ways that won't work."

In order to be able to find 10,000 ways that won't work, he must have tried 10,000 times. Do you know that GE was founded by Thomas Edison, and it is one of the oldest and the biggest enterprises in the world?

CONCLUSION

In this book I have touched upon a few traits that one way or another stop you from succeeding. This world contains infinite wisdom and what I have talked about in the book is just a drop from the vast ocean that exists amidst us.

In this book, my sole attempt has been to sensitise you towards small changes that you can bring about in your life that can open the doors for your success.

If you really think about it, there are very few physical hurdles in the world and these physical hurdles happen rarely, for example a natural calamity, or an accident that you couldn't have averted, or an attack you couldn't have foreseen.

Most of the barriers are mental. These mental barriers when not broken become mental mountains. They force you to live a limited life – they can even destroy lives for that matter in extreme cases. But the good news is, most of these mental hurdles ride on the waves of your thoughts. And if you can learn to change your thoughts, you can move these mental mountains.

This book is to get you started. It tells you what mental changes you can possibly make to initiate bigger, environmental, and even physical changes in your life.

This journey can be overwhelming for some – but you don't have to go through this journey alone.

So far, I have helped thousands of people go through mental and attitudinal changes so that they can achieve in their lives what they desire to achieve. I have helped them unclog the channels and passages that have been blocked by years of disappointments, opinions and traumas. I have climbed the mountains on my own and with the help of the wisdom I've obtained from various sources. Now I can throw you the rope if you want.

The eight traps that have been addressed in this book are the ones you must avoid.

This is my first book, and I would love to know in what ways it has helped you.

Great Mohammed Ali once said: "I am the greatest, I said that even before I knew I was."

Remember, you are what you tell yourself you are.

ACKNOWLEDGEMENT

I would like to express my gratitude to my wife who helped me through the entire journey of not just writing this book, but even through all the tough times.

I deeply thank you for your unwavering support.

MaganKa(lra)

"You can have ANYTHING in your life,

*as long as you are **willing to earn** (it)"*

- Magan K(alra)
Best Selling Author & Business Growth C(oach)

'Personal Growth leads to Business Growth' - Magan Kalra thro(ugh) his core belief has led many a people to deliver substantial results, bo(th) with people and in business.

Magan is an internationally renowned Business Growth Co(ach) acknowledged by numerous Fortune 500 companies. He has trai(ned) and coached individuals and teams across cultures in Asia, Amer(ica), Europe, Middle East and Africa to over 60 different nationalities.

In his career spanning over 20 years, Magan has redefined the (way) organizations achieve business growth by transforming the people (side) of business and has been ranked amongst the Top 10 trainers in (the) world by DC&A.

His audiences unfailingly describe his sessions as powerful, inspirati(onal) and action-oriented.

> *"You don't meet Magan. You encounter him."*
> **- PRADNYA DESHPANDE**
> Director Sales, South Asia
> Oriflame, India

> *"600+ participants and 55+ countries. It is a rare person who captures the attention, hearts, minds, energy and intellect of such numbers as Magan can. I've listened to many motivational speakers around the world and Magan is simply at the top."*
> **- PETER KROPP**
> General Manager - Europe
> Isagenix, Sweden

> *"Anything, absolutely anything is possible, this is what Magan's workshop did to me."*
> **- SANJEEWANI WEERASINGHE**
> Actress, Singer & Entrepreneur
> Srilanka

	SHORT TERM	MID TERM	LONG TERM
Impact on Business >	Happy Employees	Higher Efficiency	Business Growth
Impact on People >	Increased Motivation	Increased Effectiveness	Personal Growth

*"This was the sixth time that we used **POWERTAINMENT**™ for (our) leadership and team building events. Magan moves people out of their se(ats), gets them moving, swinging and sweating and at the same time delive(rs a) powerful message - we love it!"*

- KEDAR VA(...)
Director, Learning & Developi(ng)
Coca Cola,

MaganKalra
Now, Act

20+ YEARS

30+ COUNTRIES

60+ NATIONALITIES

1,500+ SESSIONS

1,50,000+ PARTICIPANTS

CREDENTIALS

- Author of **Success Isn't a Problem, Our Ignorance Is** and **The Success Code 2.0**
- Creator of **POWERTAINMENT**™
- Certified Global Leader of the Future
- Certified Stake Holder Centered Coach
- Certified by Landmark Education, DC&A and The Friedman Group
- Certified by NeuroLeadership Institute affiliated with ICF
- Certified analyst for variety of psychometric tools
- Certified in 'ROI Methodology'

CORPORATE TITLES

- Founder and CEO, Performance Advantage Group
- Former Vice President - The Friedman Group
- Former Head of Training with Oriflame
- Former AVP - Corporate Leadership Services with Genpact

Magan truly has a gift of customizing his message with the aspirations and objectives of his audience, comprising of high profile professionals and organizations

SPECIALIZATION

- Executive Coaching
- Leadership Development
- Personal Development
- Team Development
- POWERTAINMENT™
- Storytelling
- Presentations & Public Speaking
- Train the Trainer Certification

AUTHOR OF 'SUCCESS ISN'T A PROBLEM, OUR IGNORANCE IS'

In this book, Magan will reveal to you the unconscious and unexamined ways of being that stop us from succeeding.

The wisdom contained in this book is neither a scientific invention nor fiction. It is a conclusion based on solid empirical data and self-discovery.

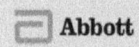

CLIENT EXPERIENCE

Clients (left sidebar): Abbott, airtel, Amway, Apollo Munich, BAYER, BIBA, Boston Scientific, Coca-Cola, CRISIL, ESTĒE LAUDER, Gerson Lehrman Group, GIORGIO ARMANI, PHILIPS, SOPHIE, TATA, TEDx, Virgin

LinkedIn
"Magan is truly inspirational and takes leaders way more a notch up. Magan is the man if you want to learn to lead."

— SANNIDHI J
Sales Performance Consultant (Asia)
Li

Nissan
"It's hard to explain what you see or learn from people. It the way they take you to places where none can. Thanks to Ma workshop, I'm brimming with positivity and creativity."

— SELEN SISMANY
Nissan,

Max Bupa Health Insurance
"Raise the Bar that was the POWERTAINMENT™ theme we used for our entire team. Magan gets you pumped up. It is high energy, full of motivation and in a bus like ours, we need it on a regular basis."

— DAMAN PAL S
Head, Quality and Business Exc
Max Bupa Health Ins

SBI Life
"Very polished, very professional, extremely prepared, it was very practical. Magan you truly lived up to the pro very powerful and very entertaining!"

— ANIL B
National Trainin
SBI Life Ins

gsk
"Magan knows how to make the needle move. If your nu are plateauing despite a great strategy and robust campaign, it's time fo to bring Magan in."

— Dr. VIVEK S
Senior M
GSK, B

Tupperware
"Magan has impacted millions of lives and how! He "learner" for life. He makes a dent in every life he encounters. Don't twice if you want to transform your life."

— SHILPA A
Managing D
Tupperwa

MaganK

www.magankalra.com
connect@performanceadvantagegroup.com
Magan would love to connect with you

f in ▶ 🐦 ⓘ

+91-9818152800

Milton Keynes UK
Ingram Content Group UK Ltd.
UKHW021633011224
451755UK00010B/596